THE
NEW CHURCH
ANTHEM
BOOK

ONE HUNDRED ANTHEMS

Compiled and Edited by
LIONEL DAKERS

Music Department
OXFORD UNIVERSITY PRESS
Oxford and New York

Oxford University Press, Great Clarendon Street, Oxford OX2 6DP, England
Oxford University Press Inc., 198 Madison Avenue, New York, NY 10016, USA

Oxford is a trade mark of Oxford University Press

First published in hardback in 1992
Paperback edition with corrections, first published in 1994
and reprinted in hardback and paperback in 1996

ISBN 0–19–353107–0 hardback
ISBN 0–19–353109–7 paperback

3 5 7 9 10 8 6 4

Printed and bound in Portugal
on acid-free paper
by Printer Portuguesa

PREFACE

When *The Church Anthem Book* first appeared in 1933 it was obviously very much a child of its time which, I imagine, is how *The New Church Anthem Book* may well be viewed in sixty or more years' time. Even so, the aims of this new collection, and the policy underlining the choice of its contents, are in no way different from the first edition which proudly proclaimed, 'The aim of this book has been to choose and assemble one hundred approved anthems old and new...'

The role of the anthem, and its place not only in parish church worship but within Christian worship generally, is as assured and as relevant today as ever. The purpose of the *The New Church Anthem Book* is to encourage the use of a wide range of reasonably simple and singable music. Where, in the old edition, organ accompaniments were unnecessarily thick, and consequently awkward to negotiate, these have been thinned out, and in a number of instances note values have been halved and bar lengths altered in the interests of musical and visual clarity. The needs of depleted or incomplete choirs, which today are very much a reality, have also been taken into account.

We have taken advantage of the wide range of scholarship which was not so readily available sixty years ago. As a result, the music of each period has been edited by an accredited scholar. What I believe we have achieved, therefore, is as accurate as possible in terms of up to the minute scholarship.

Although tastes may change, over the years they generally widen. A comparison between this book and its predecessor will reveal that about one third of the original contents have been discarded. These include most of the excerpts from oratorios, together with other examples which today seem strangely ill-assorted or irrelevant. In their place come a number of reasonably simple pieces by contemporary composers whose names have in recent years become well known and whose works are respected with good reason in church music circles.

Where no editor's name is shown against a particular piece, I am responsible for any markings shown in square brackets. These, and any other similar guidelines, all of which are intended to be as simple as possible, are consistent with current editorial practice. English singing translations have been added in many cases, but it is hoped that choirs will use the original language whenever possible. The spelling and punctuation of Tudor English texts has normally been made consistent and modernized; where, however, a twentieth-century composer has set older words with original spelling, that has been retained. There is every reason to believe that, in the late sixteenth century, organs were used to support some or all of the voice parts; performers today should therefore feel free to accompany such 'unaccompanied' anthems when appropriate.

As with any composite collection of church music spanning the centuries, a general editor cannot possibly hope to please everyone. There are bound to be inclusions and omissions which may cause some surprise, but nevertheless I believe this to be a representative collection in which the realistic needs of most average situations have been borne in mind. That is certainly my intention.

LIONEL DAKERS

CONTENTS

INDEX BY COMPOSER

SELECT LITURGICAL INDEX

Commissioned by the Chancel Choir, First United Methodist Church, Omaha, USA, for Mel Olson

1. A Gaelic Blessing

Words adapted from
an old Gaelic rune

John Rutter
(b. 1945)

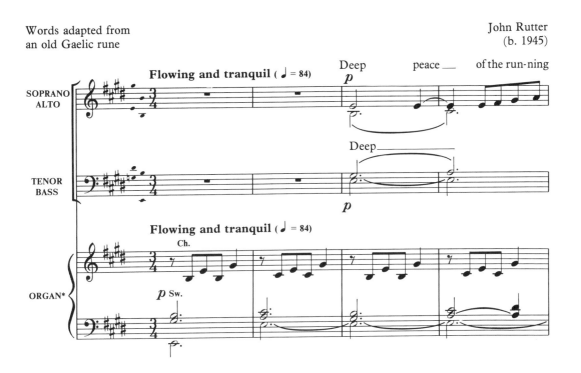

*The right hand of the organ part may alternatively be played on guitar.

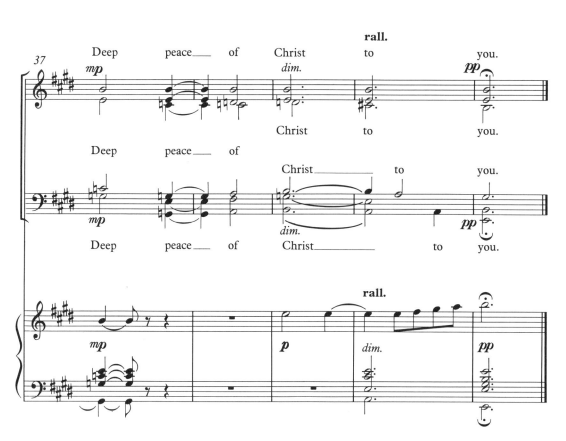

2. A Palm Sunday Antiphon

David C. Morgan
(b. 1946)

Matthew 21: 9

-san - na to the Son of Da - vid.

-san - na to the Son of Da - vid.

dim.

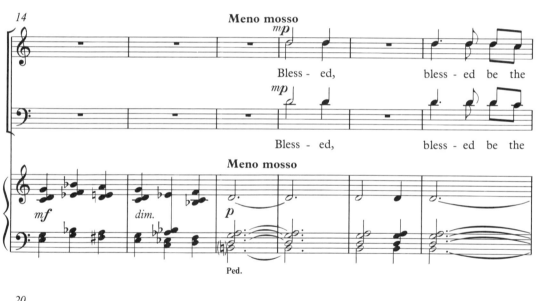

Meno mosso

mp

Bless - ed, bless - ed be the

mp

Bless - ed, bless - ed be the

Meno mosso

mf *dim.* *p*

Ped.

King, Bless - ed be the King_ that com-eth, that

King, Bless - ed be the King_ that com-eth, that

3. Above all praise

Op. 79 No. 3

Felix Mendelssohn
(1809–47)

Shortened version, adapted for SATB chorus

24

-more, Lord Thou reign - est, Lord Thou reign-est ev - er - more, for ev - er -

-more, Lord Thou reign - est, Lord Thou reign-est ev - er - more, for ev - er -

-more, Lord Thou reign - est, Lord Thou reign-est ev - er - more, for ev - er -

-more, Lord Thou reign - est, Lord Thou reign-est ev - er - more, for ev - er -

Man.   Ped.

28

-more, Hal -le -lu - jah,   Hal - le - lu - - - jah.

-more, Hal -le -lu - jah,   Hal - le - lu - - - jah.

-more, Hal -le -lu - jah,   Hal -le -lu - jah,   Hal - le - lu - - - jah.

-more, Hal -le -lu - jah,   Hal - le - lu - - - jah.

4. Adoramus te, Christe

Antiphon, Feast of the Holy Cross

Giovanni Pierluigi da Palestrina
(c. 1526–94)

All dynamics are editorial.

5. Almighty and everlasting God

Orlando Gibbons
(1583–1625)
edited by
Peter le Huray
and David Willcocks

Collect for the Third
Sunday after Epiphany

All dynamics are editorial.

6. Almighty God, which hast me brought

Thomas Ford
(c. 1580–1648)
edited by
Nicholas Steinitz

William Leighton
(fl. 1603–1614)

All dynamics are editorial.

Almighty God, which hast me brought

To Allan Wicks, in admiration, on his
twenty-fifth anniversary as Organist of Canterbury Cathedral

7. Antiphon

George Herbert
(1593–1633)

Philip Moore
(b. 1943)

The original version of this Antiphon for eight part choir is published by the RSCM.

No_ door _____ can keep __ them out;

No_ door _____ can keep __ them out;

No_ door _____ can keep __ them out;

No_ door _____ can keep __ them out;

But a-bove all,

8. Ave verum corpus

Fourteenth-century hymn, sometimes attributed
to Pope Innocent VI (d. 1342)

William Byrd
(1543–1623)
edited by
John Morehen

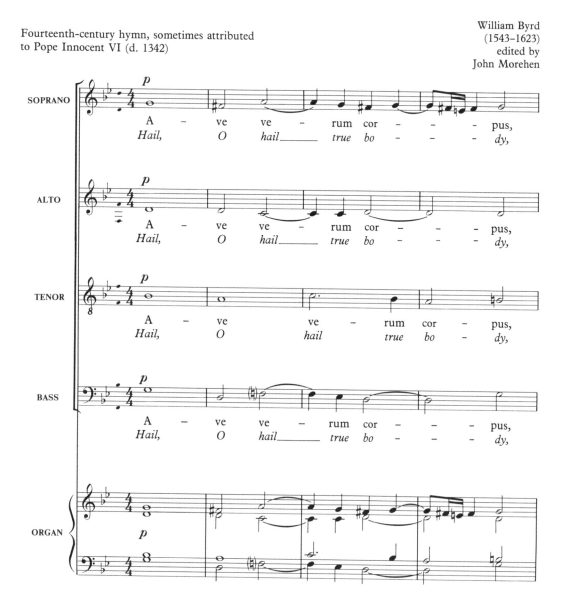

This anthem may be sung a semitone higher.

All dynamics are editorial.

9. Ave verum corpus

Op. 2 No. 1

Fourteenth-century hymn, sometimes attributed
to Pope Innocent VI (d. 1342)

Edward Elgar
(1857–1934)

10. Ave verum corpus

K618

Fourteenth-century hymn, sometimes attributed
to Pope Innocent VI (d. 1342)

W. A. Mozart
(1756–91)

All dynamics are editorial.

11. Awake, thou wintry earth

From Cantata 129
Gelobet sei der Herr, mein Gott
(Trinity Sunday)

J. S. Bach (1685–1750)
Transcribed for organ by
Richard Marlow

A - wake thou win - try earth,   Fling
De - scend - ed__ to the grave,   Where

off, fling off thy sad - ness.
our be - lov'd lie sleep - ing,

Ye ver - nal flow'rs laugh forth, laugh
Hath Christ re - turn'd to save man's

forth your an - cient___ glad - ness.
heart from woe and ___ weep - ing.

A   new and love - ly   tale   through-
O   earth, break forth and   sing,   Re -

For Gerald Knight, and composed for the Official Opening of the new Headquarters
of The Royal School of Church Music at Addington Palace, Croydon
10 July, 1954

12. Behold, the tabernacle of God

Sarum Antiphon for the
Dedication of a Church

William H. Harris
(1883–1973)

13. Blest are the pure in heart

John Keble
(1792–1866)

H. Walford Davies
(1869–1941)

Lord is theirs, Their soul is Christ's a - bode.

Still to the low - ly soul He doth him - self im - part, And

for his dwell-ing and his throne Choos - eth the pure in heart.

14. Blessed be the God and Father

I Peter

Samuel Sebastian Wesley
(1810–1876)
edited by Lionel Dakers

36
faith un-to sal-va-tion rea-dy to be re-veal-ed in the last

41
SOPRANO (SOLO)
time.   But as

Sw. Reed

45
He which hath call-ed you is ho-ly, so be ye

Man.

50
ho-ly in all man-ner of___ con-ver-sa-tion. Pass the

-o-ther with a pure___ heart___ fer - vent-ly, See that ye

love one an - o - ther, Love one an - o-ther with a

pure   heart   fer - vent-ly, a   pure_____

heart_____   fer - vent-ly, See   that ye love   one an -

15. Blessed is he that considereth

Psalm 41

Michael Wise
(1648–1687)
edited by
Christopher Dearnley

All dynamics are editorial, except where indicated.

© Oxford University Press 1992

*This dynamic is original.

16. Call to remembrance

Richard Farrant
(d. 1580)
edited by
Anthony Greening

Psalm 25: 5–6

All dynamics are editorial.

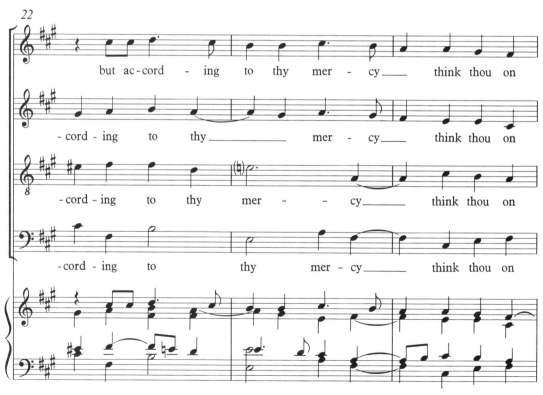

17. Cantate Domino

Psalm 148
translated by
Francis Jackson
(b. 1917)

Giuseppe Ottavio Pitoni
(1657–1743)
edited by R. R. Terry

All dynamics are editorial.

18. Come down, O Love divine

Bianco da Siena (d. 1434)
Tr. by R. F. Littledale

William H. Harris
(1883–1973)

Come down, O Love di – vine, Seek thou this soul of mine, And vis – it it with thine own ar – dour glow – ing; O Com-fort – er draw

19. Come, Holy Ghost

tr. John Cosin
(1594–1672)

Thomas Attwood
(1765–1838)
edited by Lionel Dakers

Come, Ho - ly__ Ghost, our souls in - spire, And light - en

with ce - les - tial fire. Thou the a - noint - ing Spi - rit

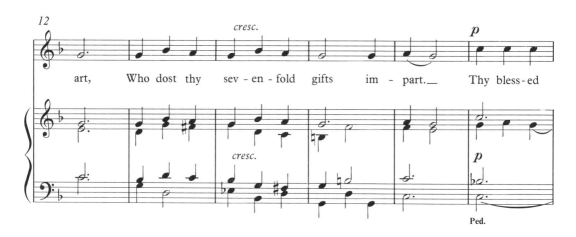

art, Who dost thy sev - en - fold gifts im - part.__ Thy bless - ed

74 a - ges all__ a - long, This__ may be__ our end - less song;

81 Praise to thy__ e - ter - nal me - rit,__ Fa - ther, Son,__ and

87 Ho - ly Spi - rit, Fa - ther, Son,__ and Ho - ly Spi - rit.

ORGAN
93

98

20. Come, ye faithful

St. John Damascene
tr. J. M. Neale

R. S. Thatcher
(1888–1957)

brought his Is – ra – el In – to joy from sad – ness;

'Tis__ the spring of souls to - day, Christ hath burst his pri -

- son, And from three days sleep__ in death As__ a sun hath

TENOR and BASS (and CONGREGATION ad lib.)

Al – – le–lu – –
Nei – ther might the gates___ of death, Nor the tomb's dark por –

– ia! Al – – le –
– tal, Nor the watch – ers, nor___ the seal, Hold thee as a

– lu – – ia!
mor – – tal; But___ to-day a – midst___ the twelve

Al – – le – lu – – ia!

Thou_ didst stand, be – stow – – ing   That   thy   peace   which

Al – – le – lu – – ia!

ev – er – more   Pass – eth   hu – man   know – – ing.

poco rit.

a tempo   **molto rit.**

ff   *fff*

21. Comfort, O Lord, the soul of thy servant

from the Anthem *Be merciful unto me*

Psalm 86: 4

William Crotch
(1775–1847)

22. Crux fidelis

Venantius Fortunatus (530–609)
Translated by J. M. Neale

John IV, King of Portugal
(d. 1656)

All dynamics are editorial.

23. Drop, drop, slow tears

Phineas Fletcher
(1582–1650)

Orlando Gibbons
(1583–1625)
arranged by D. F. R. Wilson

All dynamics are editorial.

24. Evening Hymn

H. Balfour Gardiner
(1877–1950)

Office hymn for Compline

From bars 43 to 54 inclusive the voices are to sing unaccompanied; the organ part is provided for rehearsal only.

Pro - tect _____ us, Fa - ther, God _____ a - dor'd, Thou _____ too, _____ co -
Prae - sta, _____ Pa-ter pi - is - - si - me Pa - - tri - - que

Pro - tect _____ us, Fa - ther, God _____ a - dor'd, _ Thou _____ too, __ co -
Prae - sta, _____ Pa-ter pi - is - - si - me _____ Pa - - tri - que _____

Pro - tect _____ us, Fa - ther, God _____ a - dor'd, Thou _____ too, co -
Prae - sta, _____ Pa-ter pi - is - - si - me _____ Pa - - tri - que

Pro - tect _____ us, Fa - ther, God _____ a - dor'd, Thou ___ too, _____ co -
Prae - sta, _____ Pa-ter pi - is - - si - me Pa - - tri - - que

25. Glorious and Powerful God

Op. 135, No. 3

Charles V. Stanford
(1852–1924)

Foun - der and Foun - da - tion Of end - - - less, end - less ha - bi - ta - tion.

Easter Day, 1913

26. God be in my head

Old English Prayer from *Sarum Primer*

H. Walford Davies
(1869–1941)
edited by Lionel Dakers

27. God be in my head

Old English Prayer from *Sarum Primer*

John Rutter
(b. 1945)

28. God is a spirit

from *The Woman of Samaria*

John 4: 23, 24

W. Sterndale Bennett
(1816–1875)

This anthem may either be sung accompanied or unaccompanied.

29. God so loved the world

John 3: 16, 17

John Goss
(1800–1880)

30. Haec dies

Antiphon at Vespers, etc., during
Easter week. Ps. 117: 24

Jacques Arcadelt
(b.*c.* 1510, d. 1568)
edited by John Milsom

All dynamics are editorial.

This is the day which the Lord hath made: let us rejoice and be glad therein.

31. Hide not thou thy face

Richard Farrant
(d. 1580)
edited by
Anthony Greening

Psalm 27: 10

SOPRANO: Hide not thou thy face from us, O Lord, and

ALTO: Hide not thou thy face from us, O Lord, and

TENOR: Hide not thou thy face from us, O Lord, and

BASS: Hide not thou thy face from us, O Lord, and

cast not off thy ser-vants in thy dis-plea - sure;

32. Holy, Holy, Holy

Hymn to the Trinity

Reginald Heber
(1783–1826)

Peter Ilich Tchaikovsky
(1840–1893)

To the memory of Evelyn Mary Ley

33. Holy is the true light

Translated from the
Salisbury Diurnal by
G. H. Palmer

William H. Harris
(1883–1973)

34. If we believe

I Thessalonians 4: 14, 18

John Goss
(1800–1880)
edited by Lionel Dakers

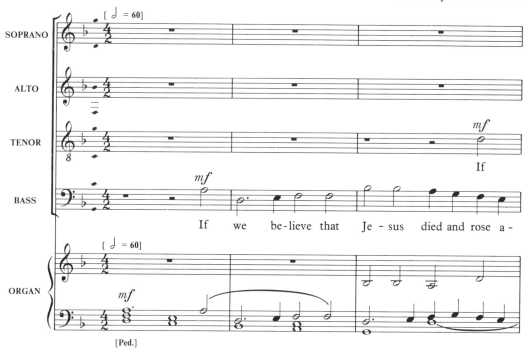

35. If ye love me

Thomas Tallis
(c. 1505–85)
edited by
Peter le Huray

John 14: 15–17

All dynamics are editorial.

36. Jesu dulcis memoria

St. Bernard of Clairvaux
Translated by J. M. Neale

Attributed Tomás Luis de Victoria
(1548–1611)

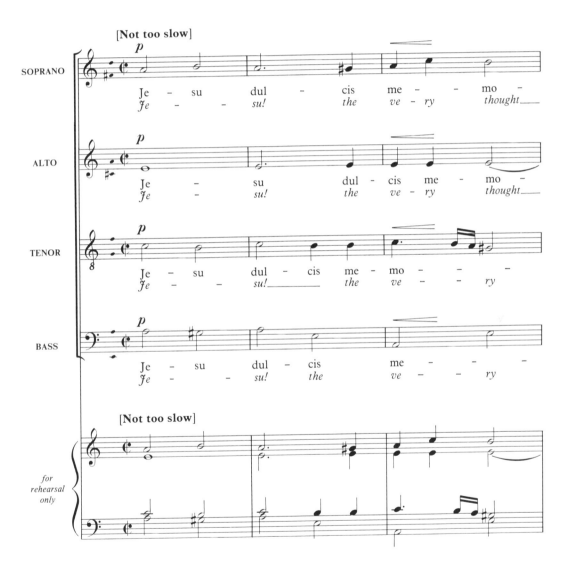

All dynamics are editorial.

37. Jesu, joy of man's desiring

from Cantata No. 147 *Herz und Mund und That und Leben*

translated by Robert Bridges
(1844–1930)

J. S. Bach
(1685–1750)
edited by H. P. Allen

38. Jesu, lead my footsteps ever
from *The Christmas Oratorio, Part IV*

English translation by
C. S. Terry

J. S. Bach (1685–1750)
Arranged by Richard D. P. Jones

Je - su,＿ lead＿ my foot - steps＿
From all＿ ills＿ my do - ings＿

All dynamics are editorial.

© Oxford University Press 1992

39. Jesu, the very thought of thee

St. Bernard
Translated by E. Caswell

Edward C. Bairstow
(1874–1946)

40. King of glory, King of peace

Jesu, meines Herzens Freud
J. S. Bach (1685–1750)
arranged by W. H. Harris
edited by Lionel Dakers

George Herbert
(1593–1632)

41. Lead me, Lord

from *Praise the Lord, O my soul*

Psalms 5: 8, 4: 9

Samuel Sebastian Wesley
(1810–1876)

42. Let thy merciful ears, O Lord

[? Thomas] Mudd
(b. *c.* 1560)
edited by W. S. Collins

Collect for the Tenth Sunday after Trinity

All dynamics are editorial.

43. Let us now praise famous men

R. Vaughan Williams
(1872–1958)
edited by Lionel Dakers

Ecclesiasticus 44

And some there be, which have no me - mo - ri - al; who are

pe - rished, as though   they had ne - ver been.   Their   bo - dies are

bu - ried in peace;   but their   name liv - eth for   e   —   ver -

- more.

44. Lo, round the throne a glorious band

Melody by N. Herman
arranged by Henry G. Ley
(1887–1962)
edited by Lionel Dakers

Rowland Hill
(1744–1833)

raise:_ Hal - le - lu - jah!

Wor - thy the Lamb, for sin - ners slain, through end - less

Wor - thy the Lamb, for sin - ners slain, through end - less

Wor - thy the Lamb, for sin - ners slain, through end - less

Wor - thy the Lamb, for sin - ners slain, through end - less

72

years___ to live   and reign: Thou hast   re -deemed us   by   thy

years   to   live___ and reign: Thou hast___ re -deemed us   by___ thy

years___ to   live   and reign: Thou hast___ re - deemed us   by   thy

years   to   live___ and reign: Thou hast   re -deemed us   by___ thy

78

cresc.

Blood,   and   made   us   kings   and priests to   God.__ Hal - le - lu -

cresc.

Blood,   and   made   us   kings___ and priests to___   God.   Hal - le - lu -

cresc.

Blood,   and   made   us   kings   and priests to   God._ Hal - le - lu -

cresc.

Blood,   and   made   us   kings   and priests to   God.   Hal - le - lu -

45. Locus iste

Gradual for the Dedication of a Church

Anton Bruckner
(1824–1896)

46. Lord, for thy tender mercy's sake

from J. Bull
Christian Prayers and Holy Meditations (1568)

Farrant* (16th c.)
edited by
Anthony Greening

*It is not possible to identify the composer of this anthem. Different sources describe the composer as 'John Hilton' and 'Farrant'. All dynamics are editorial.

47. Lord, I trust thee

from the *Brockes Passion* (1716)

Barthold Brockes
(1680–1747)
translated by
Denys Darlow

G. F. Handel
(1685–1759)
edited by
Denys Darlow

11

- ing,   For the bread of   life I'm sigh - ing.

p   [*mf*]

15 [*f*]

Quench my thirst and   let my hun - ger cease,

[*f*]

[*f*]

18

Fill my heart with   joy and end - less peace.

When the breath of life has left_____ me,

May my soul__ be blend-ed with - - thee.

For Roy Massey, David Briggs, and Hereford Cathedral Choir

48. Mary's Magnificat

Words and music by
Andrew Carter
(b. 1939)

1. Soft-ly a light is steal-ing, Sweet-ly a maid-en sings, Ev-er wake-ful, ev-er wist-ful. Watch-ing faith-ful-ly, thank-ful-ly, tend-er-ly her

49. My eyes for beauty pine

Robert Bridges
(1844–1930)

Herbert Howells
(1892–1983)

One splen - - dour thence is shed ____ from all ____ the

SOPRANO and ALTO

stars ___ a -bove: 'Tis nam - ed when God's ___ name is said, 'Tis

TENOR and BASS

poco allarg.   a tempo

Love, __ 'tis heaven - ly Love.

poco allarg.   a tempo

50. My shepherd is Lord

Words from
Pilot Study on a Liturgical Psalter

Harrison Oxley
(b. 1933)

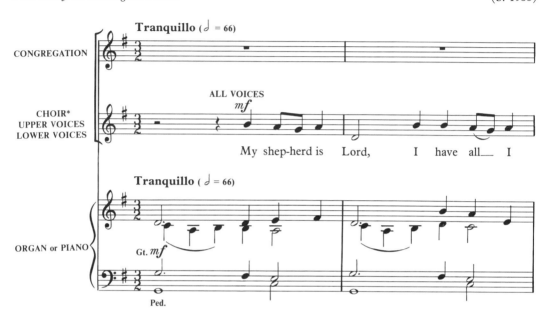

*It is not essential for the choir to divide into upper and lower voices. The setting can be sung by unison choir, lower parts and descants being omitted.

My shep-herd is Lord, I have all I need.

fields. My shep-herd is Lord, I have all I need, giv-ing me

rest in green and pleas-ant fields, re-vi-ving my

UPPER VOICES

Sw.

Man.

soul by find-ing fresh wa-ter, guid-ing my ways with a shep-herd's

*The organ part between brackets ⌐ ¬ is best omitted; this section is meant for voices unaccompanied.

*Alternative R.H. part for use when lower voices' part is omitted.

*For these two bars choir may sing with congregation if preferred.

51. My soul, there is a country

Henry Vaughan
(1622–1695)

C. Hubert H. Parry
(1848–1918)

52. Never weather-beaten sail

Thomas Campion
(1567–1620)

Charles Wood
(1866–1926)

53. Nolo mortem peccatoris

Thomas Morley
(1577/8–1602)
edited by
John Morehen

Text from a medieval carol

Translation: I do not wish the death of a sinner: these are the words of the Saviour.
This anthem may be sung a semitone higher. All dynamics are editorial.

Written for the R.S.C.M. Canterbury Area Festivals 1980

54. O come, let us sing unto the Lord

Venite, exultemus Domino

Psalm 95: 1–7

Anthony Piccolo
(b. 1953)

55. O gladsome light, O grace

translated from the Greek by
Robert Bridges
(1844–1930)

Louis Bourgeois
(c. 1510–1561)
set by Claude Goudimel
edited by Henry G. Ley

All dynamics are editorial.
This anthem may be sung unaccompanied.

56. O Holy Spirit, Lord of grace

Charles Coffin
(1676–1749)
translated by
John Chandler

Christopher Tye
c. 1505–?1572
edited by
Gerald H. Knight

All dynamics are editorial.

to F.F.

57. O how amiable

Anthem for the Dedication of a Church or other Festivals

Text from Psalms 84 and 90
and Isaac Watts (1674–1748)

R. Vaughan Williams
(1872–1958)

swal – low a nest where she may lay her young: _____ e – ven thy

al – tars, O Lord of _ hosts, my King _ and my

God. Bless – ed are they that dwell in thy _ house: _____

They will be al – way prais-ing   thee.

Poco più mosso ♩ = 100

S.A. Unis. *ff*

The glo - rious ma-jes - ty   of __ the __

T.B. Unis.

ff

Poco più mosso ♩ = 100

f   *sostenuto*   L.H.

Lord our God be up - on us: pros - per thou the __ work of our

58. O Lord, increase our faith

Henry Loosemore
(?–1670)

59. O Lord my God

King Solomon's Prayer
based on I Kings 8

Samuel Sebastian Wesley
(1810-76)
edited by
H. Watkins Shaw

Lord, for-give, Hear thou in heav'n thy dwell - ing

Lord, for-give, Hear thou in heav'n thy dwell - ing

Lord, for-give, Hear thou in heav'n thy dwell - ing

hear - est, for-give, Hear thou in heav'n thy dwell - ing

place, And when thou hear-est, Lord, for-give, And when thou

place, And when thou hear-est, Lord, for-give, And when thou

place, And when thou hear-est, Lord, for-give, And when thou

place, And when thou hear-est, Lord, for-give, And when thou

Wesley intended the first ending to be used when the treble part is sung by boys, and the second ending when it is sung by women.

60. O Lord, my God, to thee

Attributed to
Jacques Arcadelt
(*c.* 1510–1568)

From Psalms 25 & 26

All dynamics are editorial.

61. O Lord, open thou our lips

Andrew Carter
(b. 1939)

Book of Common Prayer

Responses

Spoken after the creed: The Lord be with you.
Response: And with thy spirit.
Let us pray.

Our Father

62. O Lord, the maker of all things

William Mundy
(c. 1530–91)
edited by Peter le Huray

The King's Primer 1545

All dynamics are editorial.

63. O Lorde, the maker of al thing

The King's Primer 1545

John Joubert
(b. 1927)

64. O quam gloriosum

English words by
C. Hylton Stewart
Antiphon at first Vespers,
Feast of All Saints

Tomás Luis de Victoria
(1548–1611)
edited by John Milsom

All dynamics are editorial.

65. O Saviour of the world

Antiphon at the Visitation of the Sick
(Book of Common Prayer)

John Goss
(1800–1880)

This anthem may be sung without accompaniment.

Sa-viour, Who by thy Cross and pre-cious Blood hast re-deem-ed us,

Sa-viour, Who by thy Cross and pre-cious Blood hast re-deem-ed us,

Sa-viour, Who by thy Cross and pre-cious Blood hast re-deem-ed us,

Sa-viour, Who by thy Cross and pre-cious Blood hast re-deem-ed us,

Save us, and help us, we hum-bly be-seech thee, O Lord,   we

Save us, and help us, we hum-bly be-seech thee, O Lord,   we

Save us, and help us, we hum-bly be-seech thee, O Lord, we hum-bly be-

help us, we hum-bly be-seech thee, O Lord,   we

66. O Saviour of the world

Antiphon at the Visitation of the Sick
(Book of Common Prayer)

Arthur Somervell
(1863–1937)

67. O that I knew where I might find him!

Job 23: 3, 8–9
John 20: 29

W. Sterndale Bennett
(1816–1875)

This anthem should be sung unaccompanied.

68. O thou, the central orb

Words by
H. R. Bramley

Charles Wood
(1866–1926)

Slow

SOPRANO: O thou, the cen-tral orb of right - eous love, Pure beam_____ of the most high,_____ e -

ALTO: O thou, the cen-tral orb of right - eous love,_____ Pure beam__ of the most high, e -

TENOR: O thou, the cen-tral orb_____ of right - eous love, Pure beam of the most high,_____ e -

BASS: O thou, the cen-tral orb_____ of right - eous love, Pure beam of the most high,_____ e -

ORGAN

Ped.   Man.

69. Oculi omnium

Gradual for the
Feast of Corpus Christi

Charles Wood
(1866–1926)

Adagio

SOPRANO: O - cu-li om - ni-um _____ in te _____ spe-rant

ALTO: O - cu-li om - ni-um _____ in te _____ spe-rant

TENOR: O - cu-li _____ om - ni-um _____ in te _____ spe-rant

BASS: O - cu-li om - ni-um _____ in te _____ spe-rant

for rehearsal only

SOPRANO: Do - mi - ne, _____ Do - mi - ne: _____ et tu

ALTO: Do - mi - ne, _____ Do - mi - ne: _____ et tu

TENOR: Do - mi - ne, _____ Do - mi - ne: _____ et tu

BASS: Do - _____ mi - ne, _____ Do - mi - ne: et tu

70. Panis angelicus

Camille Saint-Saëns
(1835–1921)

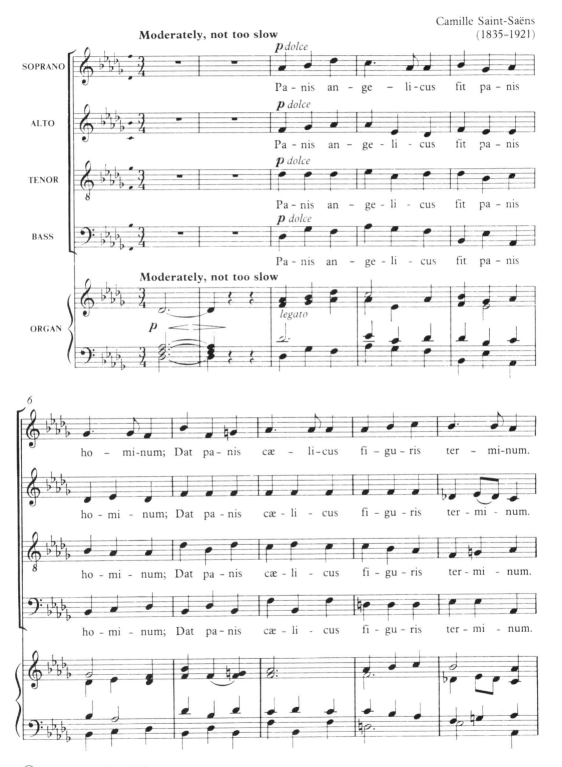

71. Praise, O praise

Sir H. W. Baker
(1821–1877)

Martin How
(b. 1931)

To be sung by all available voices. The optional lower parts may be sung by any Altos or Basses.

ev-er sure,   Praise him for our har-vest store;

He hath filled the gar-ner floor;   For_ his_ mer-cies   still en-dure

Ev-er faith-ful, ev-er sure.

And for rich-er food than this Pledge of ev-er - last-ing bliss:

†Any voices at written pitch, or an octave lower (for men) - or both, as convenient.

72. Praise to thee, Lord Jesus

Final Chorus of *St. Matthew Passion*

English translation by
Lucy E. Broadwood

Heinrich Schütz
(1585–1672)
edited by Richard D. P. Jones

All dynamics are editorial.

73. Pray that Jerusalem

C. V. Stanford (1852–1924)
edited by Lionel Dakers
Melody from
Playford's Psalms (1671)

Words from the
Scottish Psalter (1650)

74. Rejoice in the Lord alway

Henry Purcell
(*c.* 1659–1695)
arranged and edited by
Watkins Shaw

Philippians 4: 4-7

All dynamics are editorial.
String parts are available for purchase or hire from the publisher's hire library.

163

-ca - tion with thanks-giv - ing   let your re - quests be made

-ca - tion with thanks-giv - ing   let your re - quests be made

-ca - tion with thanks-giv - ing   let your re - quests be made_

167

known un - to God. And the   peace of God, which pass - eth all un-der-

known un - to_ God. And the   peace of God, which pass - eth all un-der-

known un - to God. And the   peace of God, which pass - eth all un-der-

171

-stand-ing,   shall   keep your hearts and   minds through   Je - sus Christ our

-stand-ing,   shall   keep your hearts and   minds through   Je - sus   Christ_ our

- stand -ing,   shall   keep your hearts and   minds through   Je - sus Christ our

175

Lord.   And the   peace of   God, which   pass - eth   all   un -der -stand -ing,   shall

Lord.   And the   peace of   God, which   pass - eth   all   un -der -stand-ing,   shall

Lord.   And the   peace of   God, which   pass - eth   all   un -der -stand-ing,   shall

Re – joice in the Lord al – way,   and a –gain I say, re –

Re – joice in the Lord al – way,   and a –gain I say,_____ re –

Re – joice in the Lord al – way,   and a –gain I say, re –

75. Round me falls the night

William Romanis
(1824–1899)

Melody by Adam Drese (1620–1701)
v. 1 harm. S. S. Wesley (1810–1876)
v. 2 harm. Henry G. Ley (1887–1962)
v. 3 harm. J. S. Bach (1685–1750)

76. Sacerdotes Domini

English translation by
R. R. Terry
Offertory for Corpus Christi

William Byrd
(1543–1623)
edited by John Milsom

All dynamics are editorial.

77. Salvator mundi

Antiphon at Holy Unction, Visitation
of the Sick, Book of Common Prayer

Giovanni Pierluigi da Palestrina
(c. 1526–94)

All dynamics are editorial.

78. Salve Regina
Op. 96 No. 5

Eleventh-century Marian Antiphon
English translation by John Vorrasi

William Mathias
(1934–1992)

Salve, Re - gi - na, sal - ve, Re - gi - na, Ma - ter
Hail Queen of Hea - ven, hail Queen of Hea - ven, Mo - ther

mi - se - ri - cor - di - ae: Vi - ta, dul - ce - do,___
filled with com - pas - sion mild. Source of all sweet - ness,

___ et spes nos - tra,___ sal - ve.
___ and hope of___ our___ sal - va - tion.

Ad te cla - ma - mus ex - su - les, fi - li - i He - vae.___
Oh hear our cry - ing, your child - ren ex - iled from E - den,___

416

79. Solus ad victimam

Peter Abelard
(1079–1142)
translated by
Helen Waddell

Kenneth Leighton
(1929–1988)

Let our hearts suf - fer in thy Pas - sion, Lord,__ That ve - ry suf - fer-ing

may__ thy mer - cy win._____ This is the night__ of

tears,__ the three days' space,__ Sor-row a - bi - ding of the e - ven-tide,__

Ped.

Un-til the day break with the ri - sen Christ, And hearts that sor - rowed shall be sa - tis - fied.

*So may our hearts share in thine an - guish,

Lord,___ That they may sha - rers of thy glo - ry___ be;___

*Altos may sing an 8ve lower in this phrase if desired.

80. So they gave their bodies

From Pericles' Funeral Oration (Athens 431 BC)
translated by Alfred Zimmern

Peter Aston
(b. 1938)

The words are from *The Greek Commonwealth* by Alfred Zimmern (5th ed. 1931) by permission of Oxford University Press.

35

wo — — ven, wo — ven in – to the stuff of

cresc.

cresc.

40

o – ther men's lives.

o – ther men's lives, of o – ther lives.

mf

mf

o – ther men's lives.

mf

pp

46

pp

So they gave their bo – dies to the com-mon-wealth,

pp

and re-ceived praise that will ne - ver die, that will

ne - ver, ne - ver, ne - ver die,_____ and re - ceived

praise that will ne - ver die._____

Man.

81. Subdue us by Thy goodness
from *Cantata No. 22*

Text translated from German of
Elisabeth Kreuziger, 1524

J. S. Bach (1685–1750)
arranged by Richard D. P. Jones
Chorale melody:
Herr Christ, der einig Gotts Sohn

All dynamics are editorial.

82. Super flumina Babylonis

Psalm 136 (137): 1

Orlande di Lassus
(c. 1532–94)

All dynamics are editorial.

83. Surgens Jesus

English text by
R. R. Terry

Peter Philips
(1560 or 1561-1628)
edited by Lionel Pike

All dynamics are editorial.

84. The day draws on with golden light

Aurora lucis rutilat
translated by
Thomas Alexander Lacey

Edward C. Bairstow
(1874–1946)
founded on an Angers Church Melody

To my parents

85. The secret of Christ

Text from Isaiah 42: 14–16
Revelation 22: 1–3, and
The Pilgrim Prayer (based on Colossians 4:2-4)
by the Revd Canon Derrick Walters

Richard Shephard
(b. 1949)

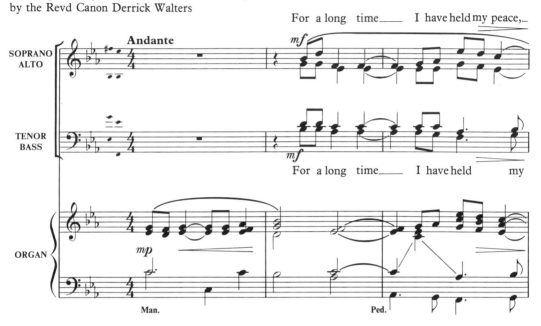

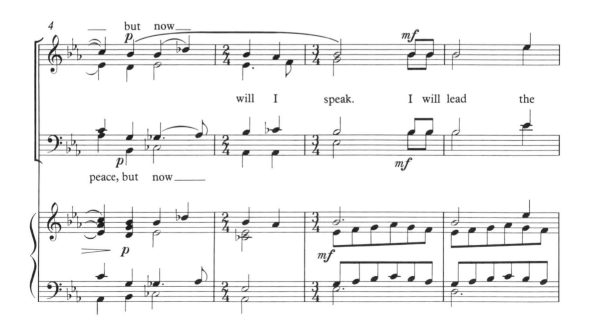

not for - sake_____ them.

And he showed me a pure ri - ver of the wa - ter of life,   clear as

cry - stal,   pro - ceed-ing out of the throne of__ God;   and on

per - se - vere   in prayer   with minds   a - wake   and

thank - - ful hearts,   that we____ may__ share   the

poco cresc.

se - cret of__ Christ   with those____ we meet   on our

unacc. ad lib.

Man.   **Ped.**

86. The souls of the righteous

Wisdom 3: 1, 2

Stanley Marchant
(1883–1949)

87. The strife is o'er

Henry G. Ley
(1887–1962)
Melody by Melchior Vulpius
(*c.* 1570–1615)
edited by Lionel Dakers

Words Anon. (18th Cent.?)
Translated by Francis Pott (1832)

*This descant is optional, and the sopranos can sing in unison with the basses if required

88. This is the record of John

Orlando Gibbons
(1583–1625)
edited by
Peter le Huray

John 1: 19

All dynamics are editorial.

unto him, What art thou? that we may give,___ that we may give an answer unto them that sent us. What sayest thou of thyself? And he said, I am___ the voice of him that crieth in the wilderness, Make straight the

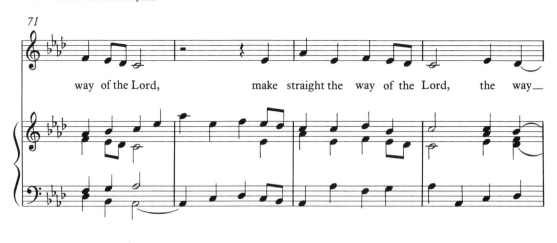

way of the Lord,   make straight the   way   of the Lord,   the   way___

S. CHORUS
And___   he said,   I   am   the voice of him___

A. 1 CHORUS
And___   he said,   I   am   the   voice___

A. 2 CHORUS
___   of   the   Lord.   And___   he   said,   I

T. CHORUS
And___   he said,   I   am   the   voice___

B. CHORUS
And___   he said,   I   am   the   voice   of

89. Thou judge of quick and dead

from 'Let us lift up our heart'

Bishop Wilberforce

Samuel Sebastian Wesley
(1810–1876)

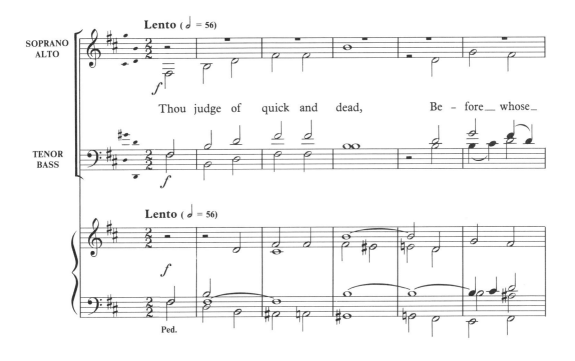

Thou judge of quick and dead, Be-fore__ whose__

bar se - vere, __ With ho - ly joy, or guilt - y dread, We

all shall___ soon___ ap‑pear; Do thou our souls pre‑pare

For that tre‑men‑dous___ day, pre‑pare for that tre‑men‑dous___

day; And fill us now with watch‑ful care, And teach our
day; And fill us now with watch – – – –

day; And fill us now with watch – ful care,___

90. Thou knowest, Lord

From the Burial Service

Henry Purcell
(1659–1695)

All dynamics are editorial.

91. Thou visitest the earth

Maurice Greene
(1695–1755)

from Psalm 65

All dynamics are editorial.

92. Thou wilt keep him in perfect peace

Isaiah 26: 3; Psalm 139: 11;
John 1: 5; Psalm 119: 175;
The Lord's Prayer

Samuel Sebastian Wesley
(1810–1876)

93. Though I speak with the tongues of men

I Corinthians 13: 1-4, 7-9, 12-13

Edward C. Bairstow
(1874-1946)

94. Turn back O Man

Melody 'the old 124th Psalm'
Arranged by Gustav Holst (1874–1934)
edited, and with organ part,
by Lionel Dakers

Clifford Bax
(1886–1962)

95. Turn thy face from my sins

Psalm 51: 9–11

Thomas Attwood
(1765–1838)

96. Wash me throughly

Psalm 51: 2-3

Samuel Sebastian Wesley
(1810–1876)

97. When Jesus, our Lord

from *Christus (Op. 97)*

Matthew 2: 1–2

Felix Mendelssohn
(1809–1847)
edited by Ivor Keys

III
CHORUS

Numbers 24: 17
Psalm 2: 9

98. When to the temple Mary went

Translated from the German by
J. Troutbeck

Johannes Eccard
(1553–1611)

All dynamics are editorial.

21
cresc.
Hope of Is - ra - el, the Hope of Is - ra - el, the
-el, the Hope of Is - ra - el, the
seen, The Hope of Is - ra - el, the Light of
the Hope of Is - ra - el, of Is - ra - el, the Light
Is - ra - el, the Hope of Is - ra - el, the Light of
Hope of Is - ra - el, the Hope of Is - ra - el, the
25
rall.
a tempo
Light of men. Help now thy ser - vants,
Light of men. Help now thy ser - vants, gra - cious
men, the Light of men. Help now thy ser - vants,
of men. Help now thy ser - vants,
men, the Light of men. Help now thy ser - vants, gra -
Light of men. Help now thy ser - vants, gra - cious

99. Where Thou reignest

Des Tages Weihe, D.763

Benjamin Webb
(1819–1885)
adapted by F. A. W. Docker

Franz Schubert
(1797–1828)

100. Zadok the Priest

After I Kings 1: 39–48

George Frideric Handel
(1685–1759)
edited by Lionel Dakers